Lost socks

Story by Dawn McMillan
Illustrations by Trish Hill

Tim and Michael
jumped into the pool.
"Here comes the ball!"
shouted Michael.

The ball made a big splash.
"Look at me!" said Mom.
"I'm all wet!"

The boys had fun.

"Please get out now, Tim,"
said his mom.
"You are getting cold.
Run inside and get dressed."

Michael's mom came to the pool.

"Look, Mom! I can swim fast," shouted Michael.

"Good boy, Michael," she said. "But you will have to get out. We have to go."

Michael went inside
to get dressed.

"I can't find my socks,"
he said.
"Where are my socks?
My socks are not **red**!"

Michael ran outside, again.
"Mom! My socks are lost,"
he said.
"I can't find my socks!"

"Come on, Michael,"

said his mom.

"We have to go and get Dad.

Come **without** your socks!"

Then Michael looked at Tim.

"I can see my white socks," he said.

Tim looked down.

"Oh, Michael!" he said.

"**I** have got your socks on."